BLOOD IN A CABIN

Real events and a revelation:
A private investigator's files

Cindy James

LEANNE JONES

PUBLISHING HOUSE

DISCLAIMER

The author/private investigator was hired by the mother of Cindy James, and the following includes her observations on this case.

While the author/investigator has tried her best to prepare the following account, no guarantee is made with respect to the completeness of the contents therein. The purpose here is to provide further information about the subject matter covered at inquest and further investigation inspired by a revelation the investigator/author experienced at inquest. The revelation led her to search to prove Cindy's claim.

The author shall have neither liability nor responsibility to any person or entity with respect to any loss or damage to character caused or alleged to be caused directly or indirectly by the information contained in this account, now or in the future. It is the expressed wish of the author that according to the findings of the 1990 inquest, which was left "undetermined," that all involved in this matter of the Cindy James case must be held blameless.

Any speculation contained herein, with respect to any of the people involved, is conjecture and was heard with contemplation and consideration of the subject matter at inquest, and based on incomplete information and inconclusive evidence. All people involved in this matter must be afforded the respect they deserve.

"It is a human desire to try to understand and look for the truth in events, especially in something so seemingly evil."

Agio
PUBLISHING HOUSE   698 Dogwood Crescent, Gabriola, BC V0R 1X4
© 2016 & 2019, Leanne Jones. All rights reserved.
Cabin illustration on cover and map on page ii by Andrew Andersen.

BLOOD IN A CABIN
ISBN 978-1-927755-77-8 (paperback)
ISBN 978-1-927755-78-5 (ebook)
Cataloguing information available from
Library and Archives Canada.

Agio Publishing House is a socially responsible enterprise,
measuring success on a triple-bottom-line basis.

10 9 8 7 6 5 4 3 2 1

REVELATION

There is a distinction between fact and truth.
Truth has an element of revelation about it.
If something is true, it does more than strike one as merely being so.

– Lucian Freud, painter, grandson of Sigmund Freud

AUTHOR'S NOTE

My name is Leanne Jones. I have always had a very strong sense of justice and the motivated energy to pursue it.

What you are about to read is the account of one cold case out of hundreds of cases I've investigated over some thirty-two years working as a private investigator. Although this case took place in the earlier part of my career, it still haunts me. I think of it often, and hope someone someday will solve the mystery.

TABLE OF CONTENTS

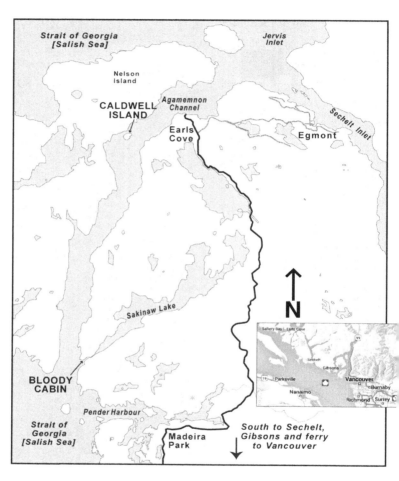

This section of the Sunshine Coast, north of Vancouver, BC, shows the key locations of the voyage taken by Cindy and Roy Makepeace, and the 'bloody cabin' site.

TIMELINE

1. **1987–1989:** Investigation into a 1979 disappearance of a young woman in the Sunshine Coast area (hired by her mother).

2. **May of 1989 onwards:** On the way back from working on that missing person case, I was staying at my mother's in Richmond when Cindy James was announced missing (May 25th), then found dead (June 8th). I investigated the nearby setting where body had been discovered. Hired to investigate by the mother of Cindy, Tilley Hack. Interviews with Drs. Anthony Marcus and Roy Makepeace, and others.

3. **1989:** Autumn 1989: Returned to Sunshine Coast for further investigation into the missing person case and talk with wharfinger Vera Grafton to verify the Makepeaces docked there on their return. Cindy's brother picked her up.

4. **February/May of 1990:** Attended the lengthy inquest into Cindy's death; evidence presented included an audio recording of a grisly 1981 murder tale revealed under hypnosis. Analyzed testimony and documents presented. Conducted some interviews. Revelation. My press release thwarted.

5. **Spring 1990:** Explored the Reid Island / Caldwell Island lead stemming from Vera Grafton's mention of taking the young man to 'Reid Island' and what was learned from the telephone call to the Bellingham owner and Pat Ling's letter. Vera took me to the Sutton Group of Islands.

6. **2004:** Learned about local tale of bloody cabin. Third investigation up to the Sunshine Coast, specifically the Lake Sakinaw area, searching for the cabin where a male and a female stayed in the early 1980s.

CHAPTER ONE

Where's Cindy?

The setting was Vancouver, Canada in the suburb of Richmond, in late May 1989.

I had just come back from the Sunshine Coast, after a second trip investigating a 1979 missing person case. I planned to stay overnight with my mother before returning home to Vancouver Island. At the time, my mother lived on Blundell Road in Richmond.

I couldn't help but get interested in something that was in the newspaper about a missing nurse. Cindy James (aka Cindy Makepeace) was last known to have deposited her paycheque at 7:59 PM on May 25, 1989 at the bank on Blundell at No. 2 Road – right across from my mother's house! Coincidentally, Cindy drove the same make and model car as mine.

I didn't think too much more about it until Cindy's body was discovered on June 8, 1989 at 8111 Blundell, just a few blocks from my mother's place. Hogtied, hands and feet bound behind her back, her body containing a lethal dose of drugs – I was drawn in. The fact the police were calling it a suicide was just too much! I was determined to find out what really happened.

Cindy's parents, Tilley and Otto Hack, lived in Sidney, so because of my proximity to many of the elements of this case, I decided to visit them. But before that, I visited the site at 8111 Blundell to take pictures and interview some people there.

[During the subsequent visit to the Hack home, I was hired by Tilly Hack for reasons only known to her but I felt it must be because she wanted some outside communication about the case. Since I had been to the scene where the body was found, I was able to tell them what I had discovered.]

Now, before I tell you about these investigations and about the revelation I received during the inquest, I would ask you to wait, and consider everything written here before coming to your own conclusions.

THE BODY OF CINDY JAMES IS FOUND

On June 9, 1989, a construction worker named Gordon Starchuk discovered the body of Cindy James on the hidden side of an abandoned house close to Number 3 Road and Blundell Road. I recorded the address as 8111 Blundell although it was abandoned with no address number on it.

I felt drawn toward looking at that site which, as mentioned, was not far from my mother's house. The newspaper said the body was found by a municipal worker from a pavement patching crew who went behind the vacant, vandalized house to relieve himself. My notes give the man's name as Gordon Starchuk.

Later I was told that Gordon was a friend to a friend of Otto Hack's grandniece whose surname was Kelm. Her father Ralph Kelm and the grandniece had worked for Dr. Roy Makepeace,

The bank where Cindy James made her last deposit before being abducted for the last time. Cindy's car was the same make, model and colour as my own. This location was a block from where I stayed at my mother's house when in Vancouver on assignments.

Abandoned house at 8111 Blundell. Cindy's body was found behind the house.

Cindy's ex-husband. If this is correct, this would just be one of many strange 'coincidences' I would uncover.

There was an ancient two-tone blue Dodge van with an old license plate parked behind the abandoned house. I thought it was derelict, however on my second visit the van had gone out and then returned while I was inside taking photos. The driver and behind-the-house camper was a man by the name of Vasily Ufimstev. I spoke to him on June 13, 1989, and this is what he said.

VASILY UFIMSTEV IN HIS VAN - WITNESS

"It was June 11th, the police had gone away when a tall, thin, balding man came around. He was also wearing glasses. He was with kids, maybe a son and two friends; one was an Indian. They smiled among themselves and asked me, 'Were you present when something happened? Was the body in there?' and they pointed at the fence. [It was the fence that blocked off the area where the body was found.] They said, 'Did you see anything?' I said, 'Better I never see anything.' Then they walked around the house to the side of the fence where the body had been found."

I wondered then if this was when the orange spray paint had been used on the oil tank that said, 'Some bitch died here.' There was also an orange outline of where the body had been, painted on the ground nearby.

When I reported Vasily's statement to the Richmond RCMP, they said, "Oh, that must have been Ozzie Kaban." Ozzie Kaban, they explained, was a private investigator Cindy had hired for protection, as she had been terrorized and physically assaulted many times over several years. I telephoned Ozzie and asked him if he was the man Vasily had described.

Ozzie replied, "I'm not balding and I'm about 300 pounds."

Later I returned to the abandoned house on Blundell and again

Vasily Ufimstev's van parked behind 8111 Blundell. It was a two-toned blue Dodge with an old license plate so initially I thought it was inoperable. However on a subsequent visit the van was out and then returned back with Mr. Ufimstev in it.

looked through the house beside where the body had been found, and took pictures and had an opportunity to look in the shed beside the house. I found some old M&S magazines and gay type magazines from San Francisco – one called *Woman for Woman*. The house was thoroughly trashed, walls and ceilings broken open and insulation scattered about. There was Heavy Metal and Satanic graffiti on the walls.

I also found, lying beside a piece of carpet, an object that looked like the end of a record player needle, when an attachment for cleaning is put on, but later I found out it was a dart. This took me in the

Interior view, showing destruction and Satanic graffiti on walls.

direction of looking into tranquilizer guns and the possibility of one of those darts being used to attack Cindy.

When I spoke to a gun specialist, he said, "Anyone wanting to bring down a person might use something like Datura or Curare. Veterinarians often used such guns and darts, and in that case they use a drug dose proportionate to the size of the animal."

Upon learning that Cindy had apparently been terrorized and abused over an extended period of time, I decided to attend a workshop on ritual abuse given by Catherine Gould, a psychologist from Los Angeles. I learned that ritual abuse had degrees of degradation. First, the use of hypnotics and massive drugs until the victim is sedated to calm them so the perpetrator(s) can do the freaky stuff. Hypnotics open the mind to indoctrination and influence. Then the perpetrator will pair drugs with acute terror at which point physical

"Some bitch died here" had been spray in orange paint on the rusted heating oil tank behind the dilapidated house. There was also an orange outline of where the body had been, painted on the ground nearby.

The dart I found inside the house. I learned this is the type of dart shot from a gun, used for tranquilizing wild animals.

pain is introduced. Putting all three of these together you have the victim susceptible to mental conditions similar to prisoners of war. More than one psychiatrist would describe Cindy as having PTSD – post-traumatic stress disorder.

I attended the workshop in August and throughout the summer I returned to the abandoned house where the body had been found, looking for clues. I found that one of the boundary stakes in front of the house where the orange paint had been used to outline the body and paint the words on the oil tank was also painted with the same color paint. A coincidence?

CHAPTER TWO

Tilley and Otto Hack

I decided to look up Cindy James's parents in Sidney. They invited me inside and told me a few details, initially in a somewhat guarded manner – and quite understandably so. Otto was a retired Lieutenant-Colonel and seemed a kind person.

They mentioned that Cindy had been married to Dr. Roy Makepeace, who was related to actor James Makepeace. They were married in 1982 and Roy lived at #1402–270 West Second Avenue, and his story is that he was also afraid about the attacks on Cindy, although the Hacks said, off the record, they had animosity toward him because at one point Cindy had confided that she thought Roy might be responsible for her harassment. The harassment took the form of strangled cats being left on her doorstep, abductions and assaults on her person, strange packages in the mail, silent telephone calls, cut phone lines, etc.

The Hacks told me Dr. Makepeace was very smooth, convincing and verbal. They described him as tall, balding, twenty years Cindy's senior. He had a violent temper, had studied to be a psychiatrist at

UBC but had failed his exams, and was engaged in a chiropractic-style 'manipulative medicine' practice at 330–5780 Cambie Street. He was in a group partnership with a Dr. King, and a massage therapist named Rich Bachman. The Hacks also thought Makepeace served as an occupational therapist who talked with people released from halfway houses.

The Hacks said that because Cindy had such fear, she privately documented the harassment over a period of years. Some incidents had been actual bodily assaults. She had been to an astrologer with Ken, her son, and the astrologer told her, "It will soon be over."

The Hacks said Cindy had finally learned to trust the city police. They also told me Cindy was a psychiatric nurse and had worked at Blenheim House, a psychiatric facility for juveniles. They said they thought Roy Makepeace was interested in voodoo and had been in some trouble with Interpol to do with guns, and he had quite a gun collection. He was also a sailing enthusiast but had sold his sailboat and now had one of two rare model Cadillacs. They wondered if he had been involved with the drug business in some way because at one time when he visited them he was looking at where they were situated near the water and had asked them what route you would take if you had to escape, that everyone should be prepared for that possibility.

They also told me about notes that Cindy had received, on her car, etc., saying things like "Soon, Cindy, soon." They said her house had been torched, the wires to her telephone had been cut, and windows broken. They said Cindy had hired Ozzie Kaban to put in an alarm system and do other duties. They said the strangest thing was that whenever the police went on surveillance at Cindy's request, nothing ever happened. Another strange thing was that even when Cindy changed her name and moved to Richmond, the threats did not stop.

The day she went missing, her groceries in bags were still in her car, and a bank card was found under the car and a receipt of deposit. When the June 9th *Vancouver Sun* reported a body found in Richmond, Otto Hack said, "I had no doubt in my mind that it was Cindy."

Before I left the Hack residence, Tilly Hack hired me, and then told me they were fixing up Cindy's house at her last address at 8220 Claysmith for sale. They said I would be welcome to accompany them to see the address whenever they went over to Richmond again. They also said Cindy had previously lived at 4780 Blenheim, 1415 West 41st Street and 334 East 40th Avenue.

Tilley and Otto Hack, parents of Cindy James. Tilley hired me to investigate Cindy's death independently of the police.

CHAPTER THREE

Dr. Roy Makepeace

I decided to interview Dr. Roy Makepeace. I just wanted to see him and gauge how he presented himself.

On Wednesday, August 9, 1989, I went to Dr. Makepeace's office having phoned two times previously. I learned that he was going away on holiday until the end of October. This time on a hunch, I told the receptionist that I was trying to get an appointment with Dr. Makepeace because he had been recommended as doing good working with prisoners. She said, "Well, he is booked up all day but he is free at the moment, maybe I can give you about two minutes."

DR. MAKEPEACE AND JONES

Makepeace: I don't know why people keep referring me when it is known that I am not taking any new patients.

Jones: **Well, no doubt it is because you are good. What is meant by manipulative medicine and is it accepted by the medical community?**

Makepeace then rambled on about the legitimacy of his field.

"Well, it's only about 10,000 years old." He started taking down textbooks and then hit upon the medical directory and told me they have a practitioner in Penticton and some on the island. It was because he was finishing his practice that he was not taking any new patients. "I'm going to Xerox this page for you."

He appeared to have a lot of nervous energy and moved fast. Initially he almost commanded me as to where I should sit in his office and he sat down near the door.

Now he was ready to complete the discussion and he rose very hastily and sped toward the Xerox room. He said, "This is my second to the last working day and then I'm going on holiday."

Not to miss the moment I said, "**Where are you going?**"

Makepeace: I'm going to be peddling thousands of miles.

Across Canada?

Well, yes, it's with that seniors cycling club and they have done media coverage of them when they went across China.

On my way out, I helped myself to the business cards on the receptionist's desk and noted that Dr. King was Dr. Makepeace's business partner and Rich Backman was the massage therapist.

I then gave the information about Dr. Makepeace's impending departure to the Hacks and telephoned the Richmond RCMP thinking they might want to keep some surveillance.

Checking at the library, I found out that manipulative medicine is the actual physical manipulation by a physician of a patient under anesthetic. Makepeace would have had convenient access to various anesthetic drugs for his practice.

CHAPTER FOUR

Psychiatrist Dr. Marcus and nurse Anne Trolson

This interview with Dr. Anthony Marcus, forensic psychiatrist, took place on July 26, 1989.

I went to a blue-roofed building on UBC [University of British Columbia] campus known as the Lloyd F. Detwiller Pavilion. I got there at 12:30 PM but the appointment was to be 1:15 so after waiting a long while, I told the people at the front desk that I had an appointment. The information person in charge went on the telephone and then said his secretary was looking for Dr. Marcus too, but rather than wait, I just went up the stairs to room 2N4. I saw the secretary, and the doctor was in a small office to the side. Looking surprised to see me, he asked me in and closed the door to the room. I mentioned that I had seen the article in the newspaper stating that he had said Cindy was engaged in a play in her private life.

I said, "**I saw it in the *Times-Colonist* Friday, July 14, 1989**

edition and Otto Hack wondered how you could do such a full assessment in 15 minutes 4 years ago?"

Dr. Marcus: I didn't like the callous way my remarks sounded in the newspaper article. I was very angry as they didn't write what I did say and they pasted together sentences. I am a forensic psychiatrist. That is one who deals with problems of law. I am called in to the RCMP Serious Crimes Unit as an independent consultant where we brainstorm together. They come to me.

In Cindy's case they gave me their history of reported incidents from 1882–85 which contained approximately 80-plus incidents. I looked at the file, and talked personally to her for one hour in December 18, 1985 after she had been found dumped on the university grounds. Then I saw her one month later for one visit of about one hour. That was when I was talking to her about what we could perhaps explore together so to take the burden off of her. I suggested she come in as a patient for peace and quiet and protection. She wouldn't do it. She was hesitant, maybe because she thought she couldn't trust. She appeared sincere, and forthright, and felt emphatically that 'THEY' had been after her and that she was being attacked by unknown persons.

In an incident in 1985, she was choked, with a black nylon stocking, disheveled and staggering.

On December 1989 when she came to the hospital, I tried to illustrate that she was involved in her own play she created, separate from her working life. Some of her reports were bizarre, some not as bizarre. Telephone lines were cut. Parcels came with strange objects in them. She said she received threatenings.

Did you ever suspect voodoo?

No, usually attacks of that type are undertaken generally by estranged lovers who have been thwarted or rejected, someone in a relationship, filled with possessive jealousy.

Someone like an estranged husband perhaps?

A possibility, he is a strange duck. I have had dealings with him on another matter.

What other matter?

I'm not prepared to say. However I at first, on hearing of her disappearance, was not surprised but thought she had created her own disappearance, and left signs of a person who had been taken away.

What about the fact that she was hog-tied?

Wasn't that just one hand to one foot?

In one of the other incidents she was pinned to the floor with her hand and it *is* possible to put a sharp thing through a hand like Christ on the cross.

What about the rape?

I don't know about that but generally the attacks were choking. What you've got to consider is could a person go to this length to perpetrate these theatricals? These attacks never happened under surveillance by Kaban.

Maybe someone harbouring deep-seeded resentment was the perpetrator.

I'm willing to keep the window open, or perhaps she cried wolf too often. The fact that didn't get across, is that the tormented self, was either from the outside or from the inside.

Who was the investigating team?

Bob Young, Gary Foster and Staff Sgt. Chris Bjornerud from Burnaby.

Did they leave the door open?

They left the door open, they actually said they should be doing more especially should the attacks result in the death or injury of the person. I had helped them look at all the possibilities. A terrorized lady is going to feel that no one believes her. I think Otto Hack believed her, in fact what was it that he said?

He said, 'How could you come to an assessment in a few minutes 4 years ago?'

I was studying the format when the newspaper came back about the disappearance. I am going to be speaking with that lady who did the article. My compassion did not come across in it and that woman said she had won a prize for journalism. Well, she can put that prize up the bum.

Well, what do you think happened to Cindy?

Well… Kaban intruded himself on her. [*This was, of course, untrue as Cindy had hired Ozzie Kaban for extra protection.*]

The police called me in. I AM interested in the answer to the puzzle.

If you look at the DSM III [*Diagnostic and Statistical Manual of Mental Disorders, edition III*] about people who can dissociate into other states. [*Marcus reads snippets*] Anger and rage…childhood trauma… somnambulism, fugue, multiple personality…

She was not psychotic, or crazy, so I always thought she did it herself basically, or someone malevolent, like other lovers, maybe Ozzie Kaban? [*He seemed to harbour some animosity to Ozzie.*]

She said 'they' were not coming to judge her; they were coming to hear… hear what? acting, theatre??

After my interview of Dr. Marcus, I read it to the Hacks and at that time I asked if Cindy had been tied one hand to one ankle and Otto Hack said, "No, both hands had been tied to both ankles behind her back. Bound three times with black silk stockings." [The black nylon theme again.] I asked for details of the body when discovered and Hack said, "The neck on her blouse had been ripped, buttons were missing. One mark was on the upper back, and a mark down her neck, deeper in the centre. Ripping at the wrist occurred, neck ripping, no eyes, no nose." [I assumed the body had been damaged by animals, insects – probably maggots at least, as two weeks had elapsed since Cindy went missing. Wasps will also eat meat, given the opportunity. I didn't ask him to elaborate.]

Mr. and Mrs. Hack said they were going to Nairobi, where their son is in the Canadian embassy. They said they would be going in August or September.

I telephoned back to Dr. Marcus to tell him about the fact that both hands were tied to both ankles. He was not in but the secretary listened and said, "Well it would be pretty hard for her to do that to herself."

Another strange occurrence happened when on January 4, 1990, I found out that Dr. Anthony Marcus lived at 2126 West 34th. I telephoned there for a Grant Marcus, thinking about the police investigator on my missing person case who had once called a Grant Marcus of Maple Ridge. Someone answered asking if I was looking for Dr. Anthony Marcus. This confirmed Dr. Marcus's address for me, but left me wondering what link there was for a Sunshine Coast policeman investigating a local woman's disappearance to be calling Dr. Marcus's home?

INTERVIEW BY TELEPHONE OF CINDY'S NURSE FRIEND, ANNE TROLSON FROM RICHMOND GENERAL HOSPITAL

Anne Trolson said, "Just before Cindy went missing, things were tense at the hospital. There was the rumor of a strike, and so there was little talk with administration.

"Cindy appeared normal; there was nothing to indicate anything out of the ordinary except she was extremely thin.

"The last time she was hospitalized last year after a bad attack, she was transferred to Richmond General. I totally believed her. Just before she went missing, her behavior was anything but abnormal, she ate with people in the cafeteria, nodding and smiling as she saw friends. She was definitely not deranged psychologically."

CHAPTER FIVE

Back to the Sunshine Coast

Autumn 1990. This was my second visit to the Sechelt area. I went to see Vera Grafton, the wharfinger at Egmont Harbour, because she was going to take me out to the Sutton island that had been for sale in 1981. Vera was a very interesting First Nations lady, and knew the missing woman personally. She lived in a small trailer and kept meticulous records about the boats coming and going from her wharf. I could see the Sutton Islands off in the distance and some of the clear-cut logging that was taking place on the other islands and far shore.

When I met Vera, I was conscious of how much better she was prepared for island exploring than I was. She was dressed in jeans, a blue jacket and rubber boots.

Vera was able to show me all of the records she kept, showing which boats docked there at Egmont. The records were stored in small individual blue notation booklets. These were arranged by year, and by date with particulars of the boats. These were important

Vera Grafton, the wharfinger at Egmont Harbour, never accepted any money for taking me out to Sutton Islands (visible in the distance). There are so many questions I wish I could go back and ask her, however Vera is now deceased. Vera had a clear view of activity on the water from her home overlooking the harbour and Sechelt Inlet.

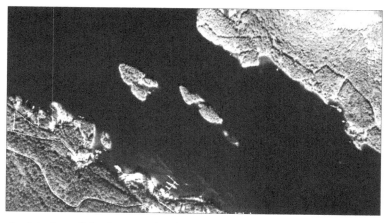

Aerial view of the Sutton Islands. The largest, heart-shaped one was for sale in 1981. The other two are almost joined at low tide.

Vera steering her boat as we leave Egmont Harbour.

The cabin on the largest Sutton Island resembles a castle.

Closer view of the cedar-shake clad exterior walls and the porch.

The wood heater did have distinctive "feet" – hard to see in this photo. There were two bedrooms as well as the kitchen/living room.

Nearby Buccaneer Marina from where Cindy and Roy Makepeace left on their fateful journey.

Log wharf structure on the beach – no longer serviceable.

documents and had been used in courts of law, she said. She told of one case, for example, where a husband and wife left after docking there at Egmont, and of how only the husband returned. This I found out was the Huber case. Later his wife's body was found and he was convicted of her murder.

[This was one of the two women reported missing at the time of Cindy's inquest at which the police detective told me, "There are no missing women from Sechelt." However there actually were two, and one was never found.]

The dock at the Bathgate's store and marina was where Vera took me from in a small motorboat out to see the Sutton Islands.

It was striking to see the cabin looking very castle-like with its crenellated roofline. The cabin/castle had two bedrooms, a stove with stubby legs, a table, a porch….

A 'For Sale' sign was prominently displayed. Also another sign that said, 'Big Snakes, Keep Off!'

On the boat ride back, Vera remarked that others had gone missing on these islands. She had taken a young man out to a 'Reid Island' and he'd disappeared too. I filed that info away in the back of my mind.

I took lots of photos on that trip, including a shot of Buccaneer Marina, which would be mentioned in a hypnosis session I'd learn about at Cindy's inquest. I also took a picture of the Pender Island health clinic where the missing woman (who was a reporter for the local newspaper) was trying to get a scoop on the fired nurses story.

CHAPTER SIX

First hypnosis sessions with Cal Booker

The Cindy James inquest turned out to be the longest and most expensive inquest in the history of BC up until that time, and resulted in an 'undetermined' verdict, leaving the case open for further investigation. It is still open to this day.

The lawyer representing the Hacks at the inquest was one of Vancouver's best, Peter Leask.

During the inquest it was revealed that Cal Booker, a hypnotherapist, was employed and paid for by Cindy James's private investigator, Ozzie Kaban, to try to learn more about three earlier alleged assaults on Cindy. There were four sessions and in the third one on the 2nd of October, 1984, came the first mention of an island incident. These sessions took place at a separate place from Ozzie's office. The final and fourth session took place in the presence of Vancouver police. Cal Booker began testimony at the inquest by claiming protection under the *Canada Evidence Act, B.C. Evidence Act*, and the *Charter*.

Booker has a Bachelor degree with a major in psychology from the University of Toronto, with hypnosis training at the Blackwell Institute in Seattle, also at Glendale, California, and with Mike Barnard who uses hypnosis in criminal investigation for the City of Vancouver Police.

His definition of hypnosis was that it is a state of relaxation and concentration. He says anyone can become a hypnotist and the Canadian Hypnosis Association is the governing body. The recognized code of ethics emphasizes that hypnosis should be beneficial, and that nothing must contravene the client's wishes. Booker said the process of hypnotizing is progressive from relaxation to a state where signs such as watering of eyes, eyelids fluttering, slowed breathing, heaviness of limbs are evident.

CAL BOOKER – 15 AUGUST 1984

The first hypnosis session took place on the 15th of August, 1984. Just three weeks previously, Cindy James had been dragged into a van (incident number 23 out of the log of incidents numbering over 80). Number 23 was logged as "July 23, 1984; attempted murder: 33rd and Dunbar park area." Ozzie Kaban had suggested the hypnotist, to help Cindy remember details.

Under hypnosis, Cindy recalled that she had been dragged into a van, given a needle in the arm. The man with a mask, no face visible, removed a wig. *[She had previously said the driver of the van was a white male with a beard and the passenger was female with long blonde hair.]* Her blouse was ripped, she woke up in bushes, she'd heard the word "hembagosh." *[Which was a word she had heard her husband Roy use. It is a Zulu word for 'carefully' as in 'hembagoshly, saquedeen' meaning 'go carefully, little boy.' I thought that there must have been two people*

Hypnotist Cal Booker conducted four sessions with Cindy for the police. At the inquest he played the recordings, including the account of a double murder committed by her husband, Roy Makepeace.

from South Africa there, since the person using the word hembagosh must have been saying it to someone who understood it.]

She overheard laughter, and gave a good description of the van in the second session on August 28th. She felt more relaxed, she said, after the last session, that she had felt good for about ten days due to post-hypnotic suggestion to assist her in her well-being, but then she had grown more fearful again and felt the world was closing in on her.

Ozzie Kaban , the private investigator and security expert hired by Cindy James during the incidents for protection. I first met Kaban at the inquest and he bought me a muffin and that was the beginning of a respect for him and his business. Later we did work for each other — and still do on occasion.

DESCRIPTION OF THE 23 JULY 1984 INCIDENT LISTED AS ATTEMPTED MURDER, AS PRESENTED AT INQUEST BY POLICE

The report was dated **July 23, 1984**. Listed as attempted murder: 33rd and Dunbar, park area at 8:30 PM.

Cindy reported to Kaban Security radio base that she would be out for about an hour, and would advise when she got home. She went to Dunbar Park, 33rd and Dunbar, with her little dog Heidi. She wandered in the park for about 30 minutes. At 9:00 PM, she looked at her watch and decided she had enough time to walk around the park and arrive home at 9:30 PM. She was walking west on 33rd Avenue, when a dark green van with a smoked window behind the passenger door, pulled alongside her. The driver of this van was a white male with a beard and the passenger was a female with long blonde hair. The driver leaned across and spoke through the passenger's window asking where Churchill Street was. The next thing Cindy could recall was being treated at the UBC hospital.

A few minutes after midnight, a neighbour at 3822 West 33rd Avenue heard someone trying to get into his front door. The door was not locked, however it had a safety chain on it. He went to the door and found Cindy trying to get in. She had black nylons tied tightly around her neck. He cut the nylons off and Cindy collapsed in the doorway. He carried her inside and called police. Shortly after that Kaban, the police and ambulance arrived. Kaban found Heidi near the front of the neighbour's house and looked after her. The neighbor is certain that Cindy did not have a dog with her at this time. He said the stocking was tied so tightly around her neck that he had difficulty getting his fingers in to cut it. He was surprised that she could breathe at all.

Kaban followed the ambulance that took Cindy to the hospital. He examined her right arm and found two recent hypodermic needle puncture marks. This was discovered in the presence of a paramedic and a nurse. No needles had been given up to this time in the hospital. She appeared to be under the influence of a drug.

Detective David Bowyer-Smyth searched the area of 33rd and Wallace. In the bush about 30 feet from the sidewalk, he found a drag mark in the earth. He also found one of Cindy's shoes, with a broken strap, and nearby he found a canister of 'Stinger' dog repellant. This had been given to Cindy by Kaban. Analysis of Cindy's blood showed the presence of a serum drug benzodiazepines. No quantitative analysis was done. Kaban located her car parked in the Dunbar Community Centre Parking lot. (Source-84/45541)

Cindy James after an attack. In this photo Cindy is 44 years old,
5 ft. 2 inches, 100 pounds.

Another hypnosis session was about the garage incident occurring on
January 27, 1983. A man came to the door of the house, rushed up,
hit her, drugged her, tied a black stocking around her neck. She tried
to telephone. She was stabbed with a paring knife. During this hypnosis session she was observed as 'quite tired, irritable, grouchy, weepy,
upset, and had a hard time coping with the information.' When asked
what was behind it, she said it was too dangerous and she wouldn't
tell anyone but God. *It was not safe: Roy told her not to tell.*

THIS INCIDENT AS DESCRIBED AT INQUEST

It was listed as taking place on **January 27th, 1983**. The time was 9:30 PM.

Cindy Makepeace was attacked in her home at 334 East 40th Avenue Vancouver. She apparently opened the back door for a male she thought was a friend. She was cut in the hand during the attack. She also had abrasions in the back and a black stocking was tied tightly around her neck, knotted three times. She was taken out to the garage where a second male was waiting. She was admitted to V.G.H. at 11:20 PM.

During investigation of this event, Cindy took two polygraph tests. The tester concluded that Cindy was not telling everything she knew. When confronted with this, Cindy advised that she had previously been approached by one of the attackers, who told her his name was 'Jimbo'. She had been holding this back because of fear.

Roy Makepeace was asked to take a polygraph test, and volunteered to take it. When the time to take the test came, the tester learned that Dr. Makepeace had medical (heart) problems, and would not be able to be tested.

Detective Bowyer-Smyth said he began the investigation of this incident feeling that Cindy had fabricated it, however, he soon changed his opinion. He said he felt it was a genuine assault on Cindy Makepeace (surname later changed to James). Source (82/67183)

DOUBLE MURDER REVEALED UNDER HYPNOSIS

On the 2nd of October, 1984, Ozzie Kaban contacted the hypnotherapist again since Cindy was experiencing flashbacks and nightmares, going back to something that had happened in June, or July of 1981. The flashbacks were a female, blood all over; Kaban suspected Cindy had walked in on a murder and wanted to get detail.

Cal Booker along with Detectives Cowan and Bjornrud, and Ozzie Kaban were present. This was a hypnosis session on January 29, 1985.

The hypnotist knew he had to regress Cindy back to a period in time before the horrific flashback scenes took place. Coming forward in time from an earlier point allowed Cindy to approach the scene without the subconscious blocks.

Gently guiding her along to the place where her memory was ready to confront the terrible event, the hypnotist appealed to her by telling her she was protected and that she would get rid of it if she could describe what happened. He gave her guidance to get to the point where she could use her memory to visualize standing in the cabin and pointing out details of the cabin and the terrible scene.

When she at first displayed reluctance, he reassured her she was protected but when she didn't believe that, he appealed to her sense of justice by asking her if she wanted the perpetrator to be loose or put in a place where he could not hurt others.

This session was conducted in a very professional manner. According to the hypnotherapist Cal Booker, her account was genuine and very descriptive.

Cindy began…
It was overcast, raining, we rowed from the club, there were no pets, we used the motor, the boat was loaded on Monday the 20th, 1981 at Thormanby Island.

Cal asked, "**Where was the dog?**"

The dog was at Doug's on Saltspring Island. *[Doug is her brother.]*

We left in the afternoon and were going to the A-frame to stay with friends but they were not there. We dropped anchor at dark. The next day was sunny, the water choppy. It was six knots. I was tanning, we stayed at Buccaneer Bay for the night. *[Buccaneer Bay is about halfway between Sechelt and Madeira Park on the Sunshine Coast.]* There was no one else. The next day, we loaded the dinghy and went in to the house, belonging to Chris and Hamish Nichol, and cleaned it up. Old Joe came by, and stayed for the day. We had a barbecue, and stayed at the cabin. It was a nice relaxed Tuesday.

Cal Booker's voice said, **"Go to Wednesday."**

Cindy: Roy rowed the boat, he took fishing gear, he wanted to look at property. We were fighting. I said, we already had property that we didn't use. We turned left out of Buccaneer Bay instead of right. We were going exploring and were going to come back that night.

Booker: **Did you come back that night?**

No.

Did you go fishing?

No.

Any fish?

No.

What did you do?

We were just driving around in the boat.

What happened?

We were relaxed, front deck, sunning.

Where going?

Nowhere in particular.

How long out?

I started feeling nauseated.

Why?

Just too much sun, water, calm.

How was Roy behaving?

He loves being on the sea.

What time did you go back?

Don't know, it was getting dark.

Anything happen?

[Long, long pause about 30 seconds.] Don't know.

Did you take any medication or pills?

Something to drink.

What drink?

A vitamin C drink, having trouble remembering. It seemed like the day didn't exist.

What do you mean?

Nothing, the fog is lifting.

It's a hot day. I should replace fluids.

How does it taste?

Bitter, fizzy.

Did you taste it before?

Just a sip.

How did it taste? Compare.

The same, it's afternoon.

Did you feel nauseous, dizzy?

[Long pause.... 15 to 20 minutes.]

How did you feel?

Dizzy, going to the cabin.

Do you recall doing that?

Felt I would pass out.

Did you make it to the cabin?

Yes!

What sounds did you hear?

Just the sounds of the room, I must have fallen asleep.

What do you recall next?

Roy came and asked me to help as he was pulling in to the property... my head felt thick.

What happened?

[.... no answer.]

How long did you sleep?

I don't know.

Were you up?

Yes.

What day is this?

The 23rd.

How do you know?

I fell asleep on the 22nd, he said we'd be there Sunday when I woke up, I thought it was the 23rd.

Move ahead now… How did you get on the island?

Some sort of log sort of thing.

Know the island?

Don't know.

Roy tell you what it was?

No, we tied to the wharf, I stayed on board, he went on to the island up the path, he did not want me to go. I didn't want to go I was afraid if I did he'd put pressure on me, he said I'd be bored as it was a gulf island. There was land to my right, not a big island, but it had houses on it. It was in a cove, there was a log wharf and rocks beside the wharf. I thought Roy was calling me.

What next?

I shouted back, waited 3 or 4 minutes, thought, waiting, jumped off, cliff part, saw a cabin made of wood, 2/3rds of a block away, log roof, walls natural, walked onto the little porch, knocked, no one came, feeling silly, uncomfortable, opened door.

What see? Take a look around… you are detached.

I must not talk about it… *[look of terror, of horror].*

You must! It is important for you to remember, nothing can keep you from remembering ….

Two people on the floor, Roy standing there… he is angry… I am scared… I can't move… shock… frozen.

Yes, do you see the two bodies?

Blood all over... blood on the knife he's got... quite a big one, five or six inches long.

It's important for you to get it all out so you can forget it...

He's not going to let me.

You can overrule others' demands.

... It's not that easy, he's very powerful. He can do whatever he wants to anyone.

Did he tell you, or did you figure this out?

It's true.

Look and describe.

The woman is on the left, brown skirt, white blouse, bare feet, average size, legs all over, lying on left side, blood under her, sprawled.

The other?

The man had on blue shorts, dark, I think boxer shorts, nothing on top, brown hair, age 30–33, girl, late twenties.

The cabin?

Little porch, two three steps to landing. Wood burning stove, squatty black little legs, big vent through ceiling, sloping roof, something left of the door, wood stacked, big axe, maps on walls, little table, rickety wooden chairs, writing paper, unfinished walls, rough flat ceiling, door to room almost shut, bathroom, little night table, two rooms, old metal beds, two pillows, white wood floor, sheets, grey blanket thrown back, paperbacks, blood on clothes.

What happened after you saw that?

Ran out, ran away.

Did he say anything?

No!

I said, 'Oh my God'... My stomach heaved, hung on to the rail, and vomited, ran down the path, he running after, he said I had to listen. He's still there, far away, he's talking, I don't want to listen.

Dr. Roy Makepeace, Cindy's estranged husband, at the inquest.
Take note, detective Bowyer-Smythe and private investigator Ozzie
Kaban knew the truth. Bowyer-Smythe was one of the finest police
detectives I have met. At inquest, they asked him to point to who he
thought was responsible for Cindy's death and he pointed directly at
Roy Makepeace. It was later when police were consulting with Dr.
Marcus that they went with the idea that she was doing all these
things to herself, that she was histrionic. That is why the tale told
under hypnosis by Cindy shocked so many people. It, along with my
own investigations, certainly convinced me. To hear the recording of
her voice and the fear that was in it was really the most chilling thing.

Is he hitting you?

Yes, across the side of the face, it's like it's foggy like I'm going
away.

Next you are on the boat

… *[No answer]* … We're going back to Thormanby Island.

What happened to the bodies?

I don't know.

See him do anything?

Big bags… throw overboard.

Bodies in bags?

I don't know… I can't talk about it.

He made you watch?

Don't want to think about it, he said. 'You're crazy, no one will believe you.'

After he cut them up, did he put in bags?

Yes!

He made you watch?

[No reply]

What did he say?

If I ever told anyone, they wouldn't believe it because he's a doctor and I'm a nobody.

Did you know he threatened David's life too [Detective David Boyer-Smith]**?**

Yes!

We believe you, why not?

I wouldn't make it up.

Did he have a saw?

Don't remember.

Did he say anything in the cabin?

I don't know, I'm sitting on the bed.

Where Roy?

Sitting beside the woman.

Is he cutting it up?

He keeps swinging the axe into parts… I can't see, I mustn't talk about it… He took blood or fluid from the bodies and rubbed it on my head and face saying if I told… the same would happen to my mother and sisters.

You don't want him doing the same to others.

Roy Makepeace (left, with unidentified couple) on his catamaran boat, circa 1981, about the time when, under hypnosis, Cindy said a double murder had happened.

I mustn't talk.

It's okay to talk, the police are here to protect.

They can't.

Feel safe?

[*No answer.*]

Do you want Roy loose or behind bars?

Not loose.

Would you like to put him there?

It's where he should be.

Will you help?

Yes!

Cindy's testimony under hypnosis was so credible to the police that a Sgt. Ferguson went out with Ozzie and Cindy in the police boat, spending one whole day looking for the scene of the double murder as described by Cindy, but they were unable to find the site. By coincidence this was the same Sgt. Ferguson who had dragged the waters around the Sutton Islands after a woman's disappearance, searching for a sunken body.

CHAPTER SEVEN

Revelation and press release

It was at this point in the inquest, hearing the dead woman's voice under hypnosis, when I realized the description of the woman in the murder scenario could easily match the missing person on my case up on the Sunshine Coast. She also owned an island. The voyage Roy and Cindy Makepeace took was up in that area.

I decided to try to attract attention to this possibility by making a press release at the inquest.

Later I found out that Dr. Makepeace often visited the medical clinic my missing person was researching for her newspaper, something to do with nurses and drugs. In further investigation I heard a statement from a local resident in Sechelt, that Dr. Makepeace's name was synonymous with drugs in the area. This however was once again a hearsay piece of information but the revelation about his association to that area would not go away.

My company Secrets Investigations is named that way for a reason. Some secrets are meant to be kept until it's the right time for them to be told. I am also the caretaker of secrets, and then again it sometimes takes a great deal of dedicated searching to unearth secrets that need to be told. This was one of those times when something revealed needed to be told in order to look for further proof to the revelation in my mind, that my missing person case and Cindy's were linked.

The reason I knew I might be right about the linkage, was when I received a death threat right after I tried to have a press release about that linkage at inquest. My assertion was dismissed at once by one of the police detectives who said definitively, "There are no missing females in Sechelt." However, he was clearly mistaken, for at that particular time there just happened to be two. One was the wife of Richard Huber, and that body was later found. And the other missing female's body has yet to be found.

Since I had been hired by Tilley Hack, mother of Cindy James, I felt it was within my right to bring a brochure detailing my investigations and theory to the inquest. I had no knowledge of the proper protocol for inquest procedure. Ozzie Kaban, the lead private investigator, asked for my brochure, as did Mr. Costello, the coroner's investigator, and police detective David Bowyer-Smyth.

At the time of the inquest in 1990, tapes of Cindy under hypnosis revealed she had witnessed her husband, Dr. Roy Makepeace, committing a double murder of a couple on an island in 1981. I thought Cindy's description of one of the murder victims could have matched my missing person. In her scenario under hypnosis, Cindy said Dr. Makepeace stopped to look at some property on an island. That voyage just happened to be up in the area close to where the missing woman had lived before she went missing. Could my missing person have still been alive and in seclusion up until 1981?

The previous summer, Corporal Jerry Anderson of the Richmond

Police, head of the Cindy James investigation, had come to see me at my mother's place because he wanted to hear what I had observed at the scene where Cindy's body had been found.

I thought I should tell him about the impression/revelation I had at inquest, that my case and Cindy's case could be linked, but since it seemed crucial to get it out quickly, I decided to give the information and theory out in the form of a press release to *The Province* newspaper during the inquest.

I wanted to give it to Salim Jiwa, the regular reporter, but since he was away I decided to release it in his absence without delay. I'd come to the conclusion that Cindy James was murdered, and while several psychiatrists had explained her behavior otherwise, Dr. Wesley Friesen gave one that seemed to fit. He said she displayed borderline personality disorder with features of PTSD – Post-Traumatic Stress Disorder. I concluded that was very likely, considering the horrific scenario she described under hypnosis. I now believed more firmly that due to information gathered on my missing person case, that the woman victim in the double murder Cindy described, might match the missing Sechelt victim. The other might have been her boyfriend since her mother said she thought the daughter was not getting along with her husband and may have had a male friend.

THE COPY OF MY PRESS RELEASE

My press release read like this:

+ February 27, 1990
+ I am a private investigator, hired by Tilley Hack, Cindy James's mother.
+ At the inquest, a brochure of my investigations was obtained by Ozzie Kaban, Mr. Costello, the inquest investigator, and detective David Bowyer-Smythe.

- At the time of the inquest, tapes of Cindy under hypnosis revealed she had witnessed a murder on an island in 1981. I worked on a missing person case up in the Sunshine Coast that seemed in my mind, to be linked to Cindy's case.

- Since that time, through further investigation, and new information, I obtained other evidence of strong links between the two cases. I compiled this information with the thought to take it to Corporal Jerry Anderson who was head of the Cindy James investigation at the time of her death in Richmond, B.C.

- As yet, I have not had the chance to give out the information but would like to give it in the form of a press release to *The Province*. I wanted to give it to Mr. Jiwa, but since he was away, and I believe it is important, I would like to put it forth at this time.

- It is my view that Cindy James was murdered, and she suffered from 'Post-Traumatic Stress Syndrome' such as was mentioned at inquest by one psychiatrist in particular. This could have been brought on from witnessing something horrific she described during the hypnosis session. The woman on my other case, missing in the Sechelt area, may have been the victim described in Cindy's hypnosis session.

Naturally this press release was not accepted into evidence because it could not be proven at the time and was not on the list of evidence compiled for the inquest. It would also upset the police theory that 'Cindy committed suicide because she was crazy.'

I hoped, naïvely, by just trying to make the release, it would draw the necessary attention resulting in further investigation and perhaps create a reasonable doubt in the police theory. The inquest went for

30 days, the last day being May 25, 1990, the first anniversary of Cindy's death.

The jury could not decide whether the manner of Cindy's death was suicide, accident or homicide so it was left as 'undetermined' although the police said they would not be re-opening their investigation. 'Undetermined' meant the inquest could be re-opened with any new investigative evidence later found.

Now after much more investigation, I will tell you what information I gathered and give you a chance to accept or reject any part of it when considering your own conclusion.

Things people told me were sometimes scrawled on restaurant serviettes or scraps of paper at hand, so this is an attempt to pull all of the data together. There are pictures and maps along with my own prospective that 'Time' sometimes provides. By doing this, I hope to give you another facet of information further to what has already been presented. The timeline this investigation and further prospective covers is approximately three decades since the actual events, but may still shed further detail about these two sad cases.

To this day the missing Sechelt person has never been found. Police checked to see if she had arrived in South Africa (as suggested by her husband); she had not. You are the detective now and you are just getting started. How did it all begin you are probably asking....

CHAPTER EIGHT

Reid/Caldwell Island, aka Deadman Island

My first motivation to interview wharfinger Vera Grafton was to verify if Cindy and Roy Makepeace had docked there because Cindy said in her account of the murder that her brother came and picked her up. Vera kept logs of boats' coming and going.

In 1990, right after the inquest, my mind kept flashing back to an incident. While on my voyage to one of the Sutton Islands with Vera Grafton, we were discussing other strange disappearances. Vera mentioned she had water-taxied a 30-ish young man who said he had to meet someone on Reid Island in Agememnon Channel. The man had disappeared, never to be found. I wondered if there could be a connection to Cindy's hypnosis story.

Searching for the island, I couldn't locate it on the Sunshine Coast charts. There was a Reid Island across the Strait of Georgia near Thetis Island, but that was way too far for a quick trip in Vera's small open boat. There was a Read Island, near Quadra Island, again many hours away across open water. After a phone call to Vera, I learned that Reid Island was a local nickname because at one point the Reid family owned it and lived there. It was apparently also called Alcatraz Island or Deadman's Island; officially it was Caldwell Island.

Vera said Pat Ling lived on Caldwell during the late 1970s. I tracked down Pat at a Chilliwack phone number. I called her and asked for as much info as she could provide.

She said she'd lived there up until January of 1980 and gave me the names of the current owners. I tracked down their contact info: Ernie and Sandy Henken (206-398-7104) who lived on Chukanut Drive in Bellingham, with Art Lawrinson (206-332-6176) of Bellingham, who was apparently part owner of a bar restaurant in Blaine called the 'International Restaurant'.

I received a letter from Pat dated April 28, 1999 in which she described the island and sent pictures. She included a floor plan sketch of the cabin. She also wrote how the Henkens used to fly up periodically, and also they and Art brought their boats up. They had a dog, a little white poodle. She also spelled Caldwell Island as Cauldwell Island.

In her letter she asked respectfully for the photos to be returned. I did not think the pictures or the description of the island and its buildings matched the account by Cindy under hypnosis. For example, the cabin had a double-width sliding glass front door. I took photocopies of Pat's pictures which, due to the time and sophistication of equipment, came out quite dark and grainy but serve as a reminder of what the photos depicted.

I have since wondered if Caldwell Island could have been for sale in 1981 (a detail provided by Cindy under hypnosis). Pat lived there only until January of 1980 and wouldn't have known; I didn't check back with the Henkens and Lawrinson.

CHAPTER NINE

Blood in a cabin

In 2004, the mother of the missing Sechelt person told me about a lady she knew who worked at Butchart Gardens near Victoria whose work was to name the flowers. This woman now lives in Brentwood Bay. She told her she once lived in a bay on Lake Sakinaw in the early 1980s. The bay (now known as Square Bay) was nicknamed 'Medic Bay' or 'Medical Bay' because so many rich doctors from Madeira Park had cabins there.

"We were referred to as the Lakers, a sort of derogatory name," she said.

Lake Sakinaw is separated from the ocean by only a small strip of land (called Sakinaw Ridge) with a creek flowing down from the lake to tidal waters. She said there was a cabin we needed to investigate, situated on the ocean side. The trail was straight across the lake from where she lived, and was alongside Sakinaw Creek, starting close to where the lake was closest to the ocean. She knew it because people liked to walk through from the lake to find oysters at the ocean.

A young couple came to live in the cabin but they didn't make the effort to get to know the Lakers so later when they disappeared no one thought anything of it and no one really cared.

Later locals found a lot of blood in the cabin but just assumed there had been an animal kill.

Sakinaw Lake is the largest lake on the Sechelt Peninsula and also the most interesting. Once connected to the ocean through its western end, its waters are separated into two layers: the top 100 feet is freshwater, while the remaining 350 are saltwater. Because all of the lighter freshwater stays in the upper layer, it is one of the warmest lakes in British Columbia, a little known fact. Surface water often reaches into the high 70s/low 80s in August! It is a gem of the Sunshine Coast; cabins stay in a family from generation to generation.

Once a map of Lake Sakinaw was located, I telephoned the lady who knew the story of blood in a cabin but she knew the cabin had since been replaced with a house. She said the blood-in-the-cabin story was common knowledge by people of the Lake Sakinaw area at the time so I decided to keep digging into my box of files and collected data, and found there was one realtor I would like to contact, who might be able to help with location since he sells property in the lake area. He also was the realtor who gave me the address that allowed me access on the missing person case to key houses in Madeira Park. His name was Bill Hunsche from Re/Max Realty.

One piece of information found while sifting through my box of data was the fact that a Sgt. Ferguson, who went with Ozzie and Cindy to look for the particular island where the double murder occurred, had coincidently also dragged the waters around an island for the missing person's body just two years previously. I learned the Staff Sgt. at RCMP Sechelt at the time was Sgt. Stelter.

I remembered Stetler was the fellow who told me the proper

protocol when going into a policing area. He said it is best to come first to the Staff Sergeant to say I would be in the area conducting investigations, instead of approaching the rookie on the desk. I took special note of that at that time and have done so ever since. However I have to admit I did learn a lot from the 'rookies' in my day.

THE CABIN AT THE A-FRAME

On June 11, 2015 at 2:10 PM, I telephoned realtor Bill Hunsche's office. Teresa Sladey telephoned back on his behalf. She said she worked in the same office as Bill.

She said when she first came up to the Sechelt area at age 16, drugs were pretty much out in the open, but all of that was now quite a bit calmer. She suggested that another realtor, Mark Chernoff, knew about Sakinaw Ridge where there was a walking path for people to come over from Sakinaw Lake to the ocean side. This was the cabin mentioned in the story as told by the mother's friend working at Butchart Gardens.

Teresa also told me she had worked for Mr. Tyner at the water board doing the invoices. Mr. Tyner was the man who had managed the medical clinic where nurses were fired over drug problems. I received heresay evidence that Dr. Makepeace was synonymous with illegal drugs in the area. He did visit that medical clinic.

Theresa also said the group of islands, one of which the missing woman and her husband had owned in the early 1980s, are officially known as the Sutton Islands.

Next I followed Teresa's suggestion and contacted Mark Chernoff who telephoned back and confirmed there had been a cabin that was removed alongside the creek at the tip of Lake Sakinaw. He said it had been removed in 1986 and people did walk through from the lake to the ocean side at that time, often for fishing and oysters. He said many ocean-going vessels at that time dropped anchor and then rowed a boat or dingy to the shore. According to some of the locals, there was often an improvised log jetty to tie up to or the boat was drawn up on shore. He did not know of a more permanent wharf.

He also said that the cabin was closer to the ocean side. These comments seemed to match the original telling of the bloody cabin story but it was a jut of land that did look somewhat like an island as in Cindy's story.

The missing person often walked from Madeira Park up to Sakinaw and apparently liked going to that lake. You could hike through the trees and get a glimpse of Agamemnon Channel.

Now that Mark helped me to pin down the fact there had been a cabin close to the trail and close to the ocean side, my attention was now once again turning toward the Sutton Island group. I was told one island was a heart-shaped one. Although Vera had taken me, I wasn't clear on which island; I mistakenly thought at first it was the one in the middle on the map. Everything has to be considered. The largest island had been for sale in summer of 1981.

I learned the middle island had been resold to a lady who I tracked down eventually; she definitely said that the largest island and first one of three, was definitely for sale in 1981. I learned the largest island was six acres and the other two, smaller ones were about two acres each.

In Cindy James's account of the voyage under hypnosis, she mentioned the 'A-frame' which might not just be an A-frame house, but could also be a triangular A-shaped section of Sakinaw Lake, near Agamemnon Channel. It was a possibility.

Then I heard back from Teresa Sladey on June 16, 2015, at 8:20 PM. Teresa Sladey wrote:

Hi Leanne:

Yes, the A-frame was a landmark (now disappeared) marking the

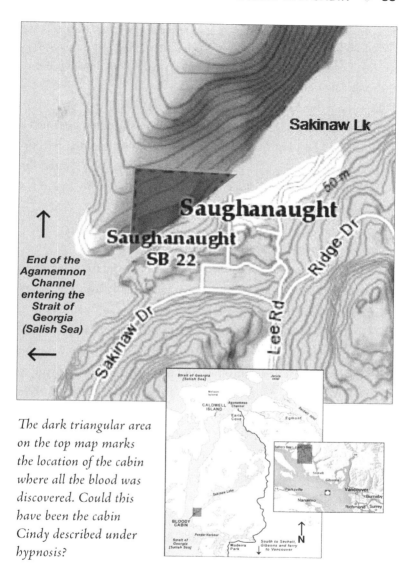

The dark triangular area on the top map marks the location of the cabin where all the blood was discovered. Could this have been the cabin Cindy described under hypnosis?

creek (Sakinaw) where it meets the ocean. My husband tells me there was originally a piece of logging equipment known as a 'donkey' with an A-frame mounted on it, used for hauling logs out of Sakinaw Lake & into the ocean.

[Please note the A-frame area in the following map.]

When Cindy mentioned going to the A-frame, she also mentioned a house owned by Hamish and Chris Nichol who were their friends. While trying to verify who Hamish and Chris were, I discovered the following obituary in *The Province* newspaper. It gave the date of his passing as August 23, 2009.

OBITUARY OF HAMISH NICHOL

Hamish Nichol was born on Christmas Day in 1924 and grew up at Ericsbery on the family farm in South Africa. He served in the Atlantic and the Mediterranean as a sub-lieutenant in the Royal Navy. After the war he moved to England to study medicine at Trinity College, Cambridge. In Birmingham and London, he studied neurology and psychiatry, before moving to New York to specialize in child psychiatry at the Albert Einstein Institute. He moved to Vancouver in 1961 where he taught psychiatry at the University of British Columbia. It was there he met his wife of 44 years, Christine. Since his retirement from UBC in 1989, he continued to work at the Pacific Voice Clinic of the Vancouver General Hospital and in private practice.

Probing a little further, I also found the obituary of Dr. Roy Makepeace shown in *The Province* newspaper.

OBITUARY OF MAKEPEACE, ROY DR.

June 8, 1926 – December 4, 2013

Passed away peacefully in Vancouver after a brave battle. He is survived by his daughters Marion and Gwen; grandchildren Jeremy, Inga and James as well as other family members and close friends. A celebration of Roy's life will be held on Saturday, December 14, 2013 from 1:00pm until 4:00pm at Brock House, 3875 Point Grey. In lieu of flowers, donations may be made to the War Amps in Roy's memory.

Researching further, I found that Dr. Roy Makepeace, M.B., Ch.B was resident in psychiatry 1964–65 at Vancouver General Hospital. In 1969 he wrote an article about the history of psychiatry in South Africa. in which he said psychiatrists had to take into consideration the Bantu psychiatric practices especially among rural Africans (mainly Zulu). This made me recall the word *hembagosh* – a Zulu word Cindy heard when she was blindfolded and abducted.

Next I wanted find out about Dr. Marcus, who was head of the UBC psychiatry section, and whose interview appeared earlier in this story, so I went looking for him and found this obituary in *The Province* as well as in the *Vancouver Sun*.

OBITUARY OF ANTHONY MARCUS

With sadness the family of Dr. Anthony Martin Marcus wishes friends and colleagues to be informed of his death on December 13, 2013. His funeral took place at the Temple Shalom Cemetery in White Rock, B.C. on December 15, 2013. Dr. Marcus was born June 21, 1929 in London, England. He was predeceased by his parents. He was educated at Cambridge University and Montreal General Hospital resulting in a doctorate in Psychiatry. Dr. Marcus joined the faculty of Medicine and Psychiatry at the University of British Columbia and was some years later made a Fellow of the Royal College of Physicians and

Surgeons. Dr. Marcus will be remembered as a noted Forensic Psychiatrist and Professor Emeritus of the University of British Columbia where he was a professor and chairman for over 30 years. Tony was broadly educated, well read, knowledgeable and ever interested and active in the Arts, travel and his Jewish heritage. He will be dearly missed by family and friends and the many patients whose lives he touched in kindness. At the end of his life he died peacefully in the Palliative Care Unit of Vancouver General Hospital after only a few days.

[Published in *Vancouver Sun* and/or *The Province* on Jan., 11, 2014.]

I noted that Makepeace and Marcus died less than two weeks apart.

A further search of published obituaries revealed that Cindy's parents are now deceased.

CHAPTER TEN

Weighing the evidence

Why did I still feel Cindy's case might be joined to the Sechelt missing person?

Here are some of the reasons:

* According to Cindy's account under hypnosis, Roy Makepeace and Cindy were travelling by ocean up into the area where at least two female and one male persons were missing.

* One female and one male persons were never found.

* Cindy talked about a double murder in a small cabin, and the description of the woman could have matched the missing woman.

* The missing person in my case had an island for sale but also liked going to Sakinaw Lake.

* Cindy said they pulled into an island, but was it an island or the tip of Sakinaw Ridge?

* One of the missing persons Vera knew said she was

planning to go to South Africa. Dr. Makepeace was from South Africa.

+ My missing woman was a reporter investigating the firing of the nurses at the Pender Harbour and District medical clinic managed by Mr. Tyner – it was rumoured to be something about drugs.

+ Dr. Makepeace visited the Pender medical clinic according to people in the area.

+ An important thing to mention is the fact that Ozzie Kaban along with Cindy and police, sailing in the police boat, spent one whole day looking for the spot Cindy described in her hypnotic state and yet they were unsuccessful in finding it. They hadn't heard of the Sakinaw blood-in-the-cabin story.

I didn't learn the 'Blood in the Cabin Story' until many years after the inquest of Cindy James but it seemed to match the story Cindy told under hypnosis. There is no definitive proof and yet it still motivated me to look for proof even several decades later. The circumstance of the life and death of Cindy James, and the mysterious disappearance of people in the Sunshine Coast area calls out for further understanding.

In closing the story of my investigations, I will say that I have presented you with my honest impressions and the details to the best of my ability of the investigations into the missing person and Cindy James cases. I always felt I was meant to be on those two cases for following reasons:

+ I had just come back from investigating in Sechelt to the murder scene in Richmond.

+ It is unusual that two cases seemed joined to each other by a revelation I had during the inquest into Cindy's death because the knowledge I had on both cases, seemed to intersect.

- It was also by strange circumstance that parents in both cases lived in Sidney, B.C. where I lived, giving me further access and availability to first-hand information.

- The other opportunity that gave me access to detail in Cindy's case was that I was staying at my mother's place two blocks from where Cindy's body was found. She had been abducted from in front of my mother's bank, sparking the curiosity that lead to my finally being hired by Mrs. Hack.

- The fact I had just returned with details from the wharfinger fresh in my mind was also relevant. The account of the voyage as told by Cindy James, under hypnosis, revealed it took place up in the same area within the time frame the woman went missing.

- The story of the blood in the cabin suggested Cindy's double murder could be true. The story at Lake Sakinaw was worth looking in on. Time went on after the Sakinaw story however, and the cabin was removed in 1986 leaving my queries once again questionable. Was the cabin's physical structure a match for Cindy's description of the murder scene?

- According to the realtors, there were a few islands for sale in 1981 at the time of the Makepeace voyage.

- There are other things to consider from the story Cindy told under hypnosis. Remember when she said she asked Roy if he wanted her to go onto the property with him, according to her he had said, "It's a gulf island and you would just be bored." Cindy also mentioned they were tied up to a long wharf and that she got off the boat by way of a 'log thing.'

✦ In my recent investigation of the area where the blood had been found in the cabin, no one could remember a wharf. However most cabins in the area had wharves of some sort.

I often believed throughout my P.I. career that there are no coincidences and some things are meant to be, however, these coincidences may be no more than steering me, which may or may not ultimately reach a provable conclusion.

This could have been one reason the inquest decision was left undetermined, however I wonder what about the proof of victimization? Out of more than eighty documented harassing actions and vicious assaults on Cindy James, only two were presented as attempt murder at inquest and then the final assault that did end in death was not considered murder. That was strange!

I wonder why was it so difficult to prove that it was murder at inquest? There definitely was proof of a body hogtied, drugged, and left behind an abandoned house. It seems that the entire system failed Cindy James, and yet so many gifted investigators were working their hearts out to help her, by trying to discover the perpetrators.

After viewing the video of Vera Grafton taking me to the Sutton Islands, I might say the cabins I saw were not the one Cindy described, however, they all have elements that agree, such as log wharves, wood stoves with stubby legs, porches, a bathroom, wooden walls. One cabin seemed castle-like. If that was where the murder took place, I wondered why Cindy did not mention its castle-like exterior. Cindy did describe the cabin as having wooden walls, but most cabins have wooden walls.

In the time of my voyage to the island in 1989, the island still had a FOR SALE sign on it but Teresa Sladey said the following: "I have been practicing real estate for 28 years in Sechelt and I am thinking that the Sutton island had been sold when I started real estate. It has since been sold twice after that." It was once sold for $440,000 and there was a foreclosure in April 17, 1990.

Now to you, the reader, it is your turn to wonder and come to your own conclusions. The case of Cindy James's death and strange harassing events still call out for more information and understanding. I feel the cases are joined but that has not yet been proven.

Perhaps you know something that could shed more light on these two significant cases?

One of the locals who owned the middle Sutton Island was clearing pathways on her property with a machete in early 1980 when she heard a shout and looked out to the inlet to see a man standing in a rowboat and calling to her, "Permission to come ashore!" Pointing, he added: "I'm from that island." He indicated the one for sale at the time.

He pulled up his boat and joined her to sit on the rocks, in the sun. She said he was moderately tall, dark and probably somewhat handsome.

She was cautious at the time because of the local rumours about his wife being missing. She said they chatted about this and that and eventually he put his head on his knee as he looked at her and said, "You feel right here." She thought it was a little presumptuous of him to make the comment but she didn't take offence.

I asked her how on Earth he could have his head on his knee and she explained: "He had his feet on a higher rock, his hands or crossed wrists on his knees, and he leaned forward and put his head down on his hands/wrists/knees and turned his head sideways to look at me when he said what he did. Quite peculiar, actually. And not something I could do myself today, being rather less flexible…."

I asked her what was her impression of his posture and

comment, and she responded: "I thought he was just trying to look cute and interesting."

After chatting for a while in a friendly way, they shook hands and he left. She never met him again

Sue Titus Reid in an excerpt from *Crime and Criminology* wrote the following: "One of the problems women faced in the 1980s and '90s and even in many cases, today, is the lack of a sympathetic and understanding attitude toward them as victims. The myth that 'she is getting what she deserves' is still held by many people. Many researchers, after studying family violence, concluded, for example, that the medical profession and social agencies are an integral part of the battered woman syndrome. They sometimes treat women as if they are crazy."

Signs of domestic abuse are ignored in many cases, and in others women are labeled psychotics or hypochondriacs and are often given prescriptions and told to go home. I think it is important that we continue reaching out to the abused instead of falling into the trap of further victimization.

WANTING TO TALK AGAIN WITH VERA

Today is June 23, 2015 and I telephoned High Tide water taxi at Backeddy Rd., Egmont, BC V0N 1N0, 604-883-9220. I told the dispatcher that Vera Grafton, the wharfinger, had driven me by boat out to the Sutton Island Group. The dispatcher was Laurie who has lived in Egmont for 30 years and knew Vera Grafton very well. She told me Vera is now deceased "as are most of the great old girls."

She also told me both the middle island and the larger island are heart-shaped.

THE SUTTON ISLANDS

I approached the Dye & Durham searching corporation to ask for a historical title search to be done. Once that was done I learned that the northernmost island was specifically known as Lot 5620. It was interesting to learn that the couple with the missing wife had owned the island from 1972 until their ownership was cancelled in 1984, and thereafter it went into the hands of five other titleholders.

Apparently as far as is known, the islands were always called the Sutton Islands, named in 1860 or so for Captain John Sutton, commander of the 74-gun British warship HMS *Egmont* when it was engaged in the Battle of Cape St. Vincent on February 14, 1797. I took note of that date (Valentine's Day!) being that the islands in question are heart-shaped.

Now I was getting interested in knowing more about the Sutton Group. I was fortunate to speak to some of the Egmont and island people from that time span. I was grateful to a previous island owner, and the lady at the High Tide Taxi who let me know that a gentleman whose wife was missing was not owner of the middle one on the map but actually the largest and first in the line but still heart-shaped. The locals said they always called them islands rather than islets. The Sechelt Islets were farther down by the Skookumchuck Narrows, which are a bit above the Sechelt Rapids.

I learned the two smaller islands were owned by women at one time and they were each about two acres. The larger one is about five or six acres. One lady bought her island from a doctor and his wife, and another lady was from the States. The doctor and his wife bought one island from an Indian family who had been there a long time. They were known to have chickens according to the locals.

The small middle island was said to have some unique underwater features as were described in diving magazines and other articles, that island was later sold to an American man from Portland Oregon.

The third and smaller island was separated from the middle

island by about 12 feet of water at high tide, forming a sort of protected swimming pool, and you could walk between the two islands at low tide.

As one islander said it was not all beer and skittles owning an island. Its insurance was expensive, which had to be purchased from Lloyd's.

Why would you need insurance, you might say? Well, mostly people went to the islands for a weekend get-away and so sometimes whenever the island was unoccupied, diggers dropped off to pillage the foreshore clams, mussels and oysters spent hours there, and islanders said that campers were a pain, breaking (not even cutting) limbs off pines to burn for campfires, therefore creating a risk for fire.

Other islanders and Egmonters from the past spoke of the joys of living even part-time on an island. One person said it like this, "To step onto land you own that is separated from neighbours, its tide pools sheltering all sorts of critters, clear deeper waters showing starfish clinging and crabs scuttling around on the bottom, hot rocks baking in the summer sun, shade trees a welcome retreat, your world supremely quiet unless a boat or plane is passing, flotsam or jetsam just waiting for you to find it as you wander the shoreline. In theory nobody can join you except at your invitation and that's a fun feeling, very relaxing!

"No cellphones in those days though, so it was literally isolated. Just a bit risky when alone, or even with a family, but when you're young…. At night the lapping water can be disconcerting initially you can wonder if the tide is coming higher than you expected, or if your boat is safely moored, but after a while you become more confident you're well above the danger zone your mind was conjuring up."

One local said she thought an island was always a special place.

Hearing thoughts about the islands took me back to what Vera Grafton said: [The missing woman] told me she was going to South

Africa and would be rendezvousing with a friend in New York." Could it be that her husband gave her a castle and a heart-shaped island, but it proved to be too isolating for such a free spirited woman?

One has to wonder if the missing woman's leaving was just as she told Vera, or did it end in the fate of a sinister nature such as the tale told by Cindy James under hypnosis?

The mysteries of life are often far stranger than fiction.

THE VICTIM

Cindy was clearly a traumatized victim. Ozzie Kaban, the lead investigator, said when he first met Cindy she was beautiful but she totally changed into a complete victim.

The question remains unanswered: who killed Cindy James?

In the appendices, you will find the lengthy incident report filed at inquest by the police. The incidents simply can't all be explained as being staged by Cindy, as Dr. Marcus hypothesized – they are too elaborate and other people must have been involved. Faced with years of harassment and violent attacks, it is difficult to imagine anyone not going crazy.

Not explained are the brief notations about Cst. Pat McBride, a policeman stationed in Cindy's house to guard her. Allegedly he was pulled off that assignment after getting into an affair with Cindy.

One theory presented at the inquest as to why Cindy was prone to being exploited by men all her life came from an uncorroborated allegation by one of Cindy's sisters that their father who was a Lt. Colonel admitted that he wasn't always generous with praise, which probably had something to do with his 35 years in the military. In an autobiographical document written by Cindy in 1986, she said as a child she was afraid of her father. "No matter how hard I tried, I never succeeded in winning his praise or approval. My father was very difficult to communicate with and ruled the household in the same way he ruled his subordinates in the air force."

Otto Hack said their parenting philosophy was to be firm, fair and love each of their six children. At inquest he said, "Cindy was sort of my favourite," and tears welled up in his eyes. It was one of the few times he showed emotion during his testimony.

In saying that personal intuition, or revelation is the way to know truth, I now have to admit this is demonstrably untrue. Personal intuition and revelation are about as reliable as guesswork when it comes to finding the truth. Revelation can be a motivator toward continued search and many things can be found, but when truth continues to remain unproven, one can only look to the biblical saying in Romans 12:19, "Vengeance is mine, sayeth the Lord." This is when something greater than ourselves becomes the continuum.

The Log of Incidents

May 17, 1966 to June 8, 1989

This 15-*page* Log of Incidents *was tabled at the inquest into the death of Cindy James. While some incidents conceivably could have been staged by Cindy (as suggested by the forensic psychiatrist Dr. Marcus), other incidents including her death seem impossible for someone to inflict on herself.*

LOG OF INCIDENTS:

17 May 66:   Cynthia Elizabeth HACK graduates Van. Gen. Hosp
              School of Nursing.

22 Jul 66:   Cynthia is registered as an RN.

9 Dec 66:   Cynthia marries Roy MAKEPEACE.

4 Jan 71:   Cynthia (Cindy) is employed at Laurel House as a
30 Jun 71:   Nurse Therapist in treatment program for children
              with behaviour problems. Left to further her
              studies. Highly recommended.

              Spent 3 years working at Children's Foundation,
              with emotionally disturbed children.

24 Apr 75:   Appointed Team Coordinator for Blenheim House.

21 Mar 82:   Cindy has minor surgery at V.G.H.
              Source - VGH medical files.

July 82:   Roy and Cindy MAKEPEACE separate. Cindy moves to
              334 E 40 Ave., and Roy remains at their home at
              1415 W 41 Ave.

14 Sep 82:   Treated V.G.H. for injury to ankle. Advised she
              tripped. Bandages & crutches.
              Source - VGH medical file.

Sept 1982:   Male in back yard, had a large roll of money in
              hand, asked for "Jimbo".
              Source - VPD flow chart & Cindy's flow chart.

7 Oct 82:   Obscene phone call. 10.00 PM
              Source - 82/67183 (P1)

8 Oct 82:   Threatening phone call. Evening.
              Source - 82/67183 (P1)

9 Oct 82:   No talk call - breathing. Mid afternoon.

              Obscene phone call. 9.00 PM.
              Source - 82/67183 (P1)

11 Oct 82:   No talk call - breathing. Mid afternoon.

12 Oct 82:   Threatening phone call. 3.15 PM.

              Obscene & threatening call. 6.00 PM.
              Source - 82/67183 (P2)

2

13 Oct 82:   Threatening phone call. 11.00 AM.

               Threatening phone call. 4.30 PM.

               Prowler. 11.59 PM.
               Separate report - Same file. Source - 82/67183 (P3)

15 Oct 82:   Rock through back door window, and entry gained.
               Nothing taken or disturbed.
               Source - 82/67183 (P3) & 82/62032

19 Oct 82:   Entry gained to house with key. Pillow on bed
               slashed and covered up with eiderdown quilt. Key
               found on bedroom floor.
               Source - 82/67183 (P4) & 82/69030

20 Oct 82:   Downstairs tenant calls police. Heard someone
               upstairs. Nothing found. 9.00 AM.
               Source - 82/67183 (P4 & 5)

29 Oct 82:   Obscene note left on back porch.
               Note not available. Ident - no prints
               Source - 82/67183 (P5)

31 Oct 82:   Pat McBRIDE moves in with Cindy. Source - Cindy's
               log & VPD flow chart.

14 Nov 82:   No talk or whispering calls. Late at night.
               Telephone number now unlisted.
               Source - 82/67183 (P6)

21 Nov 82:   Picture left on windshield of car.
               Source - 82/67183 (P6)

27 Nov 82:   No talk phone call. 10.00 PM
               Prowler on back porch. Light broken. Knocking on
               window of back door. 11.00 PM. S
               Source - 82/67183 (P7)

28 Nov 82:   **Telephone wires cut in 5 places. 10.30 PM:**
               Source - 82/67183 (P7)

1 Dec 82:   Pat McBRIDE moves out.
               Source - Cindy's Log

2 Dec 82:   No talk phone call.
               Source - 82/67183 (P7)

14 Dec 82:   Threatening letter received in mail.
               "Merry Xmas" Angie Dickenson - throat slash
               We have note. Source - 82/82604.

29 Dec 82:   Threatening letter received in mail.

4　Jan 83:		Threatening letter received in mail. McBride finds in front yard — obscene/threatening, we have note.
6　Jan 83:		No talk phone call.　7.05 PM. Source — 83/1472
7　Jan 83:		No talk phone call.　1.50 AM. Source — 83/1472 (P1)
14 Jan 83:		Harrassing phone call.　8.55 AM. Source — 83/3021 — 83/1472 (P2)
15 Jan 83:		No talk phone call.　5.10 PM.　Woman's voice in background talking over a PA system.　PC McBRIDE was presenbt when this call was received.　B.C. Tel advised the call came from the 27 exchange. (Richmond area).　Source — 83/1472 (P3)
27 Jan 83:		9.30 PM:　Cindy MAKEPEACE is attacked in her home at 334 E 40 Ave., Vancouver. She apparently opened the back door for a male who she thought was McBride.　Was cut in the hand during the attack. Also had abrasions in the back and had a stocking tied tightly around her neck, knotted 3 times. Was taken out to the garage where a second male was waiting.　Admitted to V.G.H. at 11.20 PM. During investigation of this event, Cindy took two polygraph tests.　The tester concluded that Cindy was not being entirely truthful, and was not telling everything she knew.　When confronted with this, Cindy advised that she had previously been approached by one of the attackers, who told her his name was "Jimbo".　She had been holding this back because of fear.　She declined to take another polygraph test.

Roy MAKEPEACE was asked to take a polygraph test, and volunteered to take it.　When the time to take the test came, the tester learned that MAKEPEACE had medical (heart) problems, and would not test him.

Investigator — Det. David BOWYER-SMYTH, retired — says he began the investigation of this incident feeling that Cindy had fabricated this, however, he soon changed his opinion.　He feels this was a genuine assault on Cindy MAKEPEACE (JAMES).

Source — 82/67183

28 Jan 83:		*Released from VGH at 12.15 AM.*
1 Feb 83:		*Cindy moves to 1415 W 41 Ave.* *Source — Cindy's log.*

4

8 Feb 83:   Letters were delivered to her new address, having
             been located at her old one. Threatening type.
             We have them. Source - 83/8756

11 Feb 83:   1st polygraph (not truthful) Det. V. FARMER.

18 FEB 83:   2nd polygraph (not truthful) Det. V. FARMER.

14 Apr 83:   She has received several telephone calls to this
             address since 4 Apr. PC McBRIDE was present when
             several of these calls were received.
             Threatening letter received.   We do not have
             letter. Source - 83/1472 (P3)

30 Apr 83:   Cindy moves to 3293 W 14 Ave., Vancouver.

22 Aug 83:   Letter addressed to Cindy found in outside mailbox
             of Blenheim House by secretary Denise. Letter says
             "Welcome back - death, blood, hate, etc." Letter
             destroyed by Cindy. Source - Cindy's log.

7 Sep 83:   Letter found at Blenheim House by Rena O'DONNELL at
             7.00 AM. "Cindy" pasted on outside.   Letter not
             opened. Destroyed. Source - Cindy's log

20 Sep 83:   Similar   letter found by Rena.   Not   opened,
             destroyed. Source - Cindy's log

11 Oct 83:   2 letters to Blenheim House. Not opened.
             Source - Cindy's log.

12 Oct 83:   One letter to Blenheim House. Not opened.
             Source - Cindy's log.

15 Oct 83:   Heidi barked during night. *Dead cat*, rope around
             its neck found in garden.   Note nearby "You're
             next." Source - Cindy's log to Kaban

27 Oct 83:   Garden vandalized during the night.   Flowers
             trampled and destroyed, bushes pulled out by roots,
             potted plants dumped over.   Source - Cindy's log

5 Nov 83:   Letter found on front porch by Pat McBRIDE at 8.30
             PM. Not opened. Source - Cindy's log.

9 Nov 83:   Out 6 to 8 PM. Returned to find a *dead cat* between
             2 back doors. Also a letter. Cat had been
             strangled. Source - Cindy's log - Kaban.

14 Nov 83:   Cindy hires Ozzie KABAN. Source - Cindy's log.

22 Nov 83:   Heidi finds *dead cat* near garage. Also a letter.
             Had been hit by a car not strangled.
             Source - Cindy's log - Kaban.

28 Nov 83:   Out all evening. Returned to find a letter on back porch. Source - Cindy's log.

15 Dec 83:   Two calls to Blenheim House. Apparently different male callers. Source - Cindy's log - Kaban.

20 Dec 83:   Letter to Blenheim House. To KABAN unopened. Source - Cindy's log.

23 Dec 83:   No talk call to Blenheim House. Source - Cindy's log.

31 Dec 83:   Found basement bedroom window broken. Heidi had barked at about 3.15 AM. Source - Cindy's log.

9 Jan 84:   Both back porch lights unscrewed on return from work at 5.00 PM. Source - Cindy's log.

10 Jan 84:   Awakened by Heidi barking just after 2.00 AM. Suddenly a loud thump at back of house. Tried phone, but was dead. Quiet for a while, then Heidi barked again and another loud thump at front of the house. Heidi continued to growl. Another loud thump at back. Then quiet. Cindy locked herself in her room until 7.00 AM, then went to Blenheim House and called Kaban. They checked and found phone lines cut, a basement window broken and a letter in the back. Back lights also unscrewed. Source - Cindy's log.

22 Jan 84:   Noise like metal hitting metal outside front door, then doorbell rang. Heidi barked and ran to back door. Checked both front and back - no one there. Source - Cindy's log.

24 Jan 84:   Awakened by Heidi, then doorbell rang at 3.00 AM. Found letter through front mail slot. Letter to KABAN, then given to BOWYER-SMYTH. Apparently says "blood, terror, love, death." Source - Cindy's log.

25 Jan 84:   Cindy interviewed by police - Det. BOWYER-SMYTH. She advises that there have been numerous events, including phone calls, letters, mischiefs, including 3 dead cats, and cut telephone wires. She did not report this to the police because she felt they had a low interest in her case. Got this from her "friend" PC 121 Pat McBRIDE. Source - 83/6131 (P2)

6

30 Jan 84:   Cindy was attacked at her home at 5.15 PM, by a male. She was apparently struck on the head, injected with an unknown substance, stabbed in the left hand with a paring knife, with a note stuck on the blade between her hand and the handle of the knife. She had a nylon stocking tied around her neck. Managed to radio Kaban for help at 5.50 PM. Kaban arrived at 6.05 PM, and found Cindy unconscious. Police arrived at 6.10 PM, and EHS arrived at 6.15 PM. They cut off the stocking and transported her to VGH. She did not suffer any significant head injury and had a thin red mark around her neck. She may have some damage to a tendon in her left hand. Released from hospital at 12.25 AM, 31 Jan 84. Police artist drew a composit portrait of the attacker from information supplied by Cindy. Source - 84/6236.

29 Mar 84:   Cindy undergoes a polygraph examination on above incident. Test conducted by Sgt. Cal HOOD. Cindy adjudged truthful.

24 Apr 84:   No talk telephone call.   }
                                                    }   Source - Det.
25 Apr. 84:   No talk telephone call.   }   Bowyer-Smyth's
                                                    }   notes on 84/6236
2 May 84:   Two no talk telephone calls. }   (P5)
                                                    }
8 May 84:   Two no talk telephone calls. }
                                                    }
15 May 84:   Two no talk telephone calls. }

21 May 84:   Telephone lines cut at connecting box.
              Source - 84/30799.

23 MAY 84:   At 11.00 AM, Cindy received a phone call at work. Caller advised it was Sgt. Fisk of the Vancouver Police, wanting to see her at 4.30 PM. No such person, call was false. Police staked out Cindy's house. Source - 84/6236 (P4).

31 May 84:   Threatening call at work. 2.30 PM.
              Source - 84/6236 (P4)

8 Jun 84:   Threatening call at work. 9.30 AM.
              Source - 84/6236 (P4)

9 Jun 84:   Cindy locates some fairly new stereo equipment, in the factory boxes, in her back yard. While the police are attending this incident, Roy MAKEPEACE arrives to get some items out of the garage, where he stores things. Source - 84/35308.

18 Jun 84:   Cindy arrived home from work at 5.30 PM.   At   7.30
              PM, she decided to go outside and garden. She went
              outside with her little dog "Heidi".   She left the
              back door unlocked, and open, as she probably would
              be going in and out.   She occupied herself with
              gardening,   and Heidi just wandered the   yard.   At
              about 8.30 PM, she heard Heidi bark, but felt she
              was probably barking at people on the street.   At
              9.15 PM, she called for Heidi.   When Heidi did not
              respond, she became alarmed.   She went to her
              neighbours house and called Kaban Security.   She
              did not call the police because she did not know if
              anything was wrong.   Kaban immediately dispatched
              Steve COX, who was not far from Cindy's house.   He
              instructed COX to watch the house and await his
              arrival.   Kaban arrived and found Cindy and COX
              outside,   watching   the   house.   KABAN had an
              employee, Brian LEE with him. LEE and KABAN entered
              the house through the back door.   They first found
              a 4" by 6" piece of paper on the floor just inside
              the basement door.   The note was made up of words
              cut from a newspaper.   The words were threatening
              and sexual.   There were also the words "Happy
              Birthday" on the note - Cindy's birthday had been
              six days earlier.   Further inside the house they
              found Heidi hiding under a table in a corner of the
              room.   Heidi had a string - the same type of string
              that had been around some dead cats found in
              Cindy's yard recently - around her neck.   Heidi was
              obviously in distress, so KABAN cut the string off
              her.   He noted that Heidi had been sitting in her
              own feces,   and there was more fresh feces across
              the room.   Immediately on being cut loose, Heidi
              ran to Cindy, who was still outside.
              In Cindy's bedroom, a Rothman's cigarette had been
              butted   out   on the windowsill.   KABAN feels the
              culprit was there watching Cindy from the bedroom
              window.   Cindy apparently did not smoke Rothman
              cigarettes.   Nothing was stolen, and nothing else
              was distrubed in the house.
              Source - 84/6236 (P3) 84/37410.

              KABAN and other friends advise that Heidi was very
              very close to Cindy, and they feel she could not
              mistreat the dog.   KABAN also speculates whether
              the dog would go so quickly and willingly to Cindy
              if it had been her who hurt her.   He feels this is
              a genuine incident. Source - 84/37410.

23 Jun 84:   4.00 AM: Cindy heard loud bang at rear of house, &
              saw back gate open - she always closed it.   At
              11.00 AM, dead cat found in stairwell to basement
              with string around its neck.
              Source - 84/6236 (P4) Kaban.

26 Jun 84:   Two no talk calls to work.
                  Kaban gets one no talk call at Cindy's house, while
                  Cindy is at work.
                  Source - 84/6236 (P4).

1 Jul 84:   At about 3.20 AM, Cindy gets up to answer front
                  door bell. Male, stating he is a police officer
                  wants in as there has been a prowler in the area.
                  She also sees a second male there. Asks them to go
                  to the back door, and she goes to the telephone.
                  Finds it is dead (wires have been cut). Men did
                  not go to the back door. Cindy summons help by
                  calling Kaban on radio he has provided.
                  Source - 84/40249 84/6236 (P5).

6 Jul 84:   Threatening call at work - gave name Greg LIHAN or
                  LINER. Source - 84/6236 (P5).

9 Jul 84:   Cindy is asleep in her bedroom upstairs. Her
                  mother, Matilda HACK is asleep in the basement bed-
                  room. At about 2.30 AM, the dog began barking.
                  Mrs. HACK woke up to hear Cindy walking around -
                  she had gotten up to check the doors and windows.
                  HACK then heard a loud "thump" sound, and then was
                  joined by Cindy in the basement bedroom. They BOTH
                  then heard the front doorbell ring once. They both
                  went upstairs and discovered damage to a front
                  window. The window appeared to have been struck by
                  someone standing on the front porch. It was
                  cracked in concentric rings, but was not broken out
                  of the frame. No missile was found near it. Cindy
                  attempted to call police, but found the phone dead.
                  The lines had been cut again.
                  Source - 84/6236 (P5) 84/42001.

11 Jul 84:   4.00 PM: Cindy in front yard. Dog barked, she
                  looked between houses and saw a man run north
                  through a neighbour's yard. Source - 84/6236 (P5).

15 Jul 84:   Dog barked and Cindy heard a bang at the bedroom
                  window. 1.45 AM Cindy heard running at the side of
                  the house. 2.30 AM, doorbell rang, no one there.
                  3.00 AM, Cindy looked out the window and saw a
                  silver car parked behind Cindy's car. Saw a man in
                  the road walk to Cindy's car, stopped by the door
                  of Cindy's car, looked toward the house and waved.
                  Appearance reminded Cindy of man from 11 July 84.
                  10.30 AM, Kaban tried to phone, phone wires were
                  cut. Sources - 84/6236 (P5).

19 Jul 84:   1.30 & 1.50 AM, no talk calls. 1.20 PM, call at
                  work, threats. Source - 82/6236 (P6).

23 Jul 84:   <u>ATTEMPTED MURDER:</u> 33rd & Dunbar - park area.
At 8.30 PM, Cindy reported to Kaban Security radio
base that she would be out for about an hour, and
would advise when she got home. She went to Dunbar
Park, 33rd & Dunbar, with Heidi. She wandered in
the park for about 30 minutes. At 9.00 PM, she
looked at her watch and decided she had enough time
to walk around the park and arrive home at 9.30 PM.
She was walking west on 33 Ave, when a dark green
van with a smoked window behind the passenger door
pulled alongside her. Driver of this van was a
white male with a beard and the passenger was a
female with long blonde hair. The driver leaned
across and spoke through the passenger's window
asking where Churchill Street was. The next thing
Cindy could recall was being treated at UBC
Hospital.
A few minutes after midnight, Mr. Regan TRETHEWEY,
of 3822 W 33 Ave heard someone trying to get into
his front door. The door was not locked, however,
it had a safety chain on it. He went to the door
and found Cindy trying to get in. She had nylons
tied tightly around her neck. He cut the nylons
off and Cindy collapsed in the doorway. He carried
her inside and shortly after that the police and
ambulance arrived. Mr. TRETHEWEY is certain that
Cindy did not have a dog with her at this time. He
says the stocking was tied so tightly around her
neck that he had difficulty getting his fingers in
to cut it. He was surprised that she was able to
breath at all.
KABAN followed the ambulance that took Cindy to the
hospital. He examined her right arm and found 2
recent hypodermic needle puncture marks. This was
in the presence of a paramedic and a nurse. No
needles had been given to Cindy up to this time.
In the hospital, she appeared to be under the
influence of a drug.
Det. BOWYER-SMYTH searched the area of 33rd and
Wallace. In the bush about 30 feet from the
sidewalk, he found a drag mark in the earth. He
also fouund one of Cindy's shoes, with a broken
strap, and nearby he found a canister of "Stinger"
dog repellant. This had been given to Cindy by
KABAN. Analysis of Cindy's blood showed the
present of a serum drug benzodiaepines. No
quantitative analyses was done. KABAN found Heidi
near the front of TRETHEWEY's house, and looked
after her. Also located car parked in the Dunbar
Community Centre parking lot.
Source - 84/45541.

10

24 Jul 84:   Lisa LATTIMORE at UBC Hospital receives a telephone
                call from male with accent asking questions on
                hospital security, staffing, hours, etc. Played
                tape of Roy MAKEPEACE talking. Strong possibility
                that the voice is the same.
                Source - 84/45541 Statement on file.

25 Jul 84:   *Discharged from UBC Hospital.*

15 Aug 84:   First session of hypnosis. Arranged by O. KABAN.

21 Aug 84:   *Investigation turned over to Det. K. BJORNERUD of
                Major Crime Section.*

28 Aug 84:   Second session of hypnosis.

2 Oct 84:   Third session of hypnosis. First mention of island
                incident.

12 Dec 84:   Threatening letter received.

22 Dec 84:   Telephone lines cut.
                Large fresh tracks found in snow found by police.
                Source - 84/84784

28 Dec 84:   Telephone lines cut.
                Fresh snow on ground, no footprints
                Source - 84/85966

29 Jan 85:   Final session of hypnosis. Witnessed by Vancouver
                Police. Recalls incidents of July 81 on a remote
                island.

29 May 85:   Telephone lines cut.

4 Apr 85:   Threatening telephone call.

21 Jun 85:   *Cindy admitted to Lions Gate Hospital under MHA.
                Is very depressed and suicidal. Name Cindy JACOBS
                is used.*

26 Jun 85:   *Released from Lions Gate Hospital to care of her
                brother Doug. Leaves against medical advise.*

28 Jun 85:   Telephone lines cut.

2 Jul 85:   Vancouver Police start intensive **stake out** at
                Cindy's home. Is a 24 hour stake out utilizing up
                to 14 men. Cindy is aware of this.
                Source - S/Sgt. BJORNERUD.

9 Jul 85:   **Stake out** is terminated.
                Source - S/Sgt. BJORNERUD.

//

10 Jul 85:   Cindy reports getting a no talk phone call.   Has
              tape   recorder   on telephone.   Police and   BC   Tel
              investigation   show   that   Cindy   dialed   her   own
              number.   Source – S/Sgt K. BJORNRUD.

11 Jul 85:   Mail   received – book "Blood Flowing Freely" and   a
              black   nylon   received by Cindy.   Book traced   to
              purchase at Banyen Books, 2685 W Broadway.
              Source – S/Sgt. BJORNRUD.

12 Jul 85:   Threatening phone call at work.
              Source – S/Sgt. BJORNERUD.

19 Jul 85:   At 29th and Dunbar, male driver, 25-35 years, dark
              hair   and mustache & beard called Cindy's name   and
              make finger across throat gesture.
              Whispering telephone call at work.
              Source – S/Sgt. BJORNERUD & VPD Flow chart.

27 Jul 95:   Mail received – black plastic cosmetic case
              containing meat. Source – 83/6131.

5 Aug 85:   *Phone lines cut, basememt window forced open.   No*
              marks   on   window,   dust & cobwebs   not disturbed.
              Photos were taken.   Source – S/Sgt BJORNERUD.

21 Aug 85:   Arson   fire in basement   bathroom.   Window   forced
              open,   same   as on 5 Aug,   and 6 fire starts   – no
              accellerant found.   Apparently pieces of   burning
              paper were spread around the bathroom.   Window was
              a small one,   hinged along the bottom.   Examination
              from   outside showed tall grass around   the   window
              was undisturbed, and dust and cobwebs on the window
              sill   and   frame   were   also   undisturbed.   Det.
              HALLIDAY   formed opinion that there was no way   the
              window was forced from outside. Source – 85-54932.

8 Sep 85:   Phone call – "On fire!" 7.08 PM.   Call came from
              Steveston exchange. Source – VPD log.

24 Sep 85:   Alarm goes off. Source – 85/5002.

11 Nov 85:   Two calls. Source – S/Sgt. Bjornrud report 2/12/85.

18 Nov 85:   Two calls. Source – S/Sgt. Bjornrud report 2/12/85

12

1 Dec 85:	*Cindy moves to Richmond - 5400 Blundell Rd. Vancouver Police send investigator to Richmond RCMP to familiarize them with their investigations. Source - Sgt. K. HOLMBERG.*
	Ozzie KABAN advises Richmond RCMP that Cindy has moved to their area. He advises them that Dr. Makepeace has beat her and stabbed her. He is considered armed and dangerous. Source - RCMP #83/32170
11 Dec 85:	At about 6.00 PM, 11 Dec 85, JAMES was seen staggering along beside the road on 16 Ave., near the University grounds. She collapsed into a ditch. Assisted. Had a black nylon stocking around her neck. Taken to University Hospital. Was swollen and bruised around left eye, lacerations to right fingers, bruise around her neck, abrasions on her knees, her left shin, and her left forearm, as well as a needle mark on her right inner elbow. Cindy is very poor on details of what happened to her. She worked as usual during the morning at Blenheim house, and went to lunch on Dunbar St. While walking back from lunch, she stopped at a drug store and picked up a prescription. Is unsure what happened after this. At hospital, she is being interviewed by Det. Carol Ann HALLIDAY, and is very groggy, almost incoherant, when, she points to her inside left elbow and says that a needle mark was not there before. She has 3 needle marks. Two were the result of treatment at the hospital. Blood analysis shows no drugs that would cause her problems. Source - VPD 85-79799.
19 Dec 85:	*Released from UBC Hospital.*
22 Dec 85:	To Germany. Source - Calander.
10 Jan 86:	Returns from Germany. Source - Calander
12 Mar 86:	Divorce judgement by way of Decree Nisi. Source - Cindy's papers.
2 Apr 86:	Attempt B. & E. Rear window removed. Alarm set off. Source - 86-8783.

13

16 Apr 86: Arson fire. Considerable damage to downstairs room located at the front of house. Cindy, Tom and Agnes WOODCOCK, and dog Heidi all made it out safely. All occupants asleep. Cindy awakened at about 2.30 AM by Heidi barking and a thump. Looked out bedroom window and saw flames coming out the downstairs window. Rushed to awaken WOODCOCKs. Telephone not working. Used Kaban's "panic button" which did not work, then attempted to set off burglar alarm, which again did not work. Ran to next door neighbour to call fire department. After fire was extinguished and cooled down, investigators ascertained that the fire was started from inside the residence. Apparently there were no burn marks on the rug to indicate something had been thrown in from outside, and there was no evidence of a break-in. There were 2, and possibly 3 hot spots. The 2 most noticeable were on each side of the curtain, directly below same. Police formed the opinion that Cindy was responsible for this fire. Source – 86-10276.

April 86: Asked by landlady to vacate 5400 Blundell. Source – Cindy's papers.

2 May 86: Admitted to St. Pauls Hospital. Poor health due to not eating. Suicidal.

5 May 86: Admitted to Riverview.

20 May 86: Transferred Riverview to St. Pauls.

25 Jun 86: Divorce by way of Degree Absolute granted. Source – Cindy's papers.

15 Jul 86: Released from St. Pauls. Stayed with friends until she left for Germany.

28 Jul 86: To Germany. Source – Calander.

25 Aug 86: Return to Vancouver. Source – Calander. Lived at W. 14 Ave house.

3 Sep 86: Offer made on house at 8220 Claysmith, accepteed.

18 Oct 86: House at 3293 W 14 Ave is sold.

20 Oct 86: Legal name change from Cynthia Elizabeth MAKEPEACE to Cindy JAMES. Source – Cindy's papers.

17 NOV 86: Fired from job at Blenheim House. Is on full salary. Source – Cindy's papers.

29 Nov 86: Cindy moves to 8220 Claysmith Rd., Richmond, B.C.

14

28 Jun 87: Alarm set off. Cindy was away at the time. Police
feel wind caused alarm to go off.
Source- R.C.M.P. #87/20595.

28 Aug 87: Attempt B. & E. Rear window broken, alarm set off.
Source - 87/28295.

21 Aug 87: Attempt B. & E. Rear basement window pried. Outside lightbulb unscrewed. Source - 87/28700.

6 Sep 87: Attempt B. & E.   Window in rear basement door cut
with a glass cutter and popped out. Alarm set off,
rear outside lightbulb loosened.   Glove impression
on bulb. Source - 87/29450.

11 Feb 88: Attempt B. & E.   Electrical tape put on window of
rear basement door and window   broken,   alarm
activated.   JAMES advises investigators of 2 other
attempt B. & E.s in the past 3 weeks that she has
not reported. Source - 88/4174.

11 Oct 88: Roy MAKEPEACE gets first phone call on answering
machine. "Cindy, dead meat soon".

12 Oct 88: Roy MAKEPEACE gets second phone call on answering
machine. "Hey man ......".

26 Oct 88: ATTEMPTED MURDER: 8220 Claysmith Rd., Richmond.
Cindy arrived home from work at Richmond General
Hospital at about 8.30 PM.   She sat in her car for
several minutes in her carport to make sure everything was safe. Opened the door to get out and was
grabbed from behind.   Apparently passed out. Re-
gained consciousness shortly after midnight long
enough to activate her panic button which raised
the alarm. Found unconscious by police half in and
half out of her car. She was nude from waist down,
had a black nylon stocking around her neck, and was
"hog-tied", arms and legs, with a second black
nylon. Source - 88-34989.

26 Jan 89: Mr. Ton GROENEVELT, a friend of Cindy's was found
dead in his car in front of Cindy's house.   Death
was due to a heart attack and no foul play
suspected.   Ton was in his 70s, with a history of
heart problems.   He had been visiting Cindy the
evening before.   He and Cindy had played bridge
with Tom and Agnes WOODCOCK.   The WOODCOCK's had
stayed overnight after Ton had left. His death was
apparently quite a shock to Cindy.
Source - Coroner's file available. 89/213/0147

15

8 Apr 89:	Note found on Cindy's car in Richmond General Hospital parking lot, by security guard. Note said "Soon Cindy." At end of her shift, saw "Sleep Well" written in dew on windshield. Words were written backwards so Cindy could read them when inside the car. We have copy of note. Source - 89/19492 & 89/10499.
9 Apr 89:	Alarm activated. Rear basement window insecure, note left. Rear outside light loosened. Dogmaster states no one had been in back yard. Source - 89/10609.
22 Apr 89:	Alarm while Cindy at work. Rear basement window broken. Neighbour outside when alarm went off, saw nothing. Another neighbour saw window broken that morning. Source - R.C.M.P. 89/12231.
29 Apr 89:	Attempt B. & E. Rear window broken and alarm activated. Source - 89/12974.
10 May 89:	Attempt B. & E. Kitchen window pried and alarm activated. Lightbulb loosened. Source - 89/14357.
25 May 89:	**CINDY GOES MISSING. Last seen walking from bank machine at bank at No. 2 Rd., and Blundell.** Source - 89-16241.
8 Jun 89:	**CINDY'S BODY IS FOUND - NO. 3 RD AND BLUNDELL.**

More Photographs

From one of the longest ever inquests

in BC court history

These three photos show Satanic type graffiti at the house where Cindy was found dead.

Corporal Jerry Anderson led the task force to find the missing Cindy James in Richmond. He visited me at my mother's apartment. I told him about the man in the van saying there was a tall, grey-haired man with glasses and three kids — one an Aboriginal — who asked him if he had seen anything.

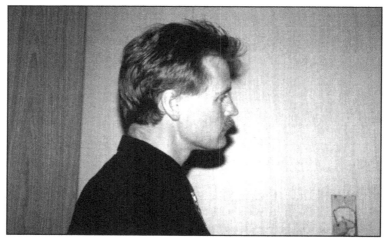

Detective Bjornrud, the police investigator who said definitively, "There are no missing persons in the Sechelt Sunshine Coast area."

The high-powered (and expensive) defence lawyer for the Hacks (Cindy's mom and dad) who hoped the inquest would declare a 'murder'.

44398837R00056

Made in the USA
Middletown, DE
10 May 2019